That Old Black Garlic of Mine in Hell

Best Recipes

Keith Pepperell

Copyright © 2016 Keith Pepperell

All rights reserved.

ISBN-13: 978-1530048908
ISBN-10: 1530048907

DEDICATION

As always to my spawn Jack, Lydia, and Alexandra all of whom are no strangers to black garlic, the gentlefolk of Woollard End, and dreadful indentured servitude at Donovan's Pub and Restaurant, Galena, Ohio.

ACKNOWLEDGMENTS

Lady Estima Davenport

Mr. Leslie Merkin

Mrs. Misaki Fong

Amitrasudan 'Ernie' Bhagwat

Muriel Dinwiddy

Sidney 'Porky' Widgeon

Quimbush Merkin

The Gentlefolk of Woollard End

Ye Olde Black Pig

Jason Horn (Cover Image)

Statestreet (Image Indian Street Food)

That Old Black Garlic Has Me In Its Spell

THE RECIPES

Lady Estima Davenport's Black Garlic Mayonnaise

Lady Davenport (81) is a long-time resident of Woollard End in the delightful county of Suffolk in

England. During World War II (the second unpleasantness) she and her old school chum and tennis partner Muriel Dinwiddy (nee Fotheringay) both cracked the enigma code and overpowered an evil gang of escaping Nazi war criminals using only kitchen paraphernalia. Many time Senior Ladies Doubles Champions at The All English Club (or Wimbledon to the less informed) the plucky pair had recently prevailed again having beaten the plucky Dutch pairing of Mrs. Tieten Van Der Tepels en Miss Snavel Klootwijk, the German team of Mrs. Behaard Verbrand und Miss Hinken Hahn and the ever popular Swedish pairing of Miss Stygg Nipplar and Mrs. Enorma Skinka-Vind in a thrilling final.

Lady Davenport's former housekeeper, the serial murderess Janet Frobisher, was highly regarded in the county of Suffolk for both her homicidal disposition and her delightfully moist Victoria Sponge Cakes.

That Old Black Garlic Has Me In Its Spell

She was terribly fond of black garlic and had recently tunneled out of a maximum security penal institution using only an attractively engraved sterling silver jam spoon.

She is still on the lam.

This recipe was given to Lady Davenport by Nadezhda Sergeevna Alliluyeva second wife of Iosif Vissarionovich Dzhugashvili better known as Joe 'laughing boy' Stalin and was slighly changed by Lady Davenport by her removing the instructions which required those naughty bourgeoisie supplying the ingredients transported to gulags in small unmarked vans.

Ingredients:

6 naughty black garlic cloves (carefully peeled)

3 free-range large brown eggs (use nice yolks only)

2 level teaspoons freshly squeezed Meyer lemon juice

One half teaspoon kosher or nun blessed salt

1 cup extra virgin or rarely ever naughty olive oil

A very small sprinkle of nicely ground pink peppercorn

Method:

In a smallish mixing bowl toss in garlic cloves, egg yolks, ground pink peppercorn sprinkle and kosher or nun blessed salt.

Whisk and blend together gently enough to incorporate nicely the soft black garlic but not so violently as to get tennis elbow. Lady Davenport frequently employs her gardener, the local reprobate Mr. Septimus Sachs, to do the whisking and also a modern electric stick whisk can be employed by those of a lazy disposition.

While continuing to whisk, begin to slowly drizzle in the olive oil. It will begin to thicken nicely so slowly continue adding the olive oil until it has reached a lovely, slightly thick mayonnaise consistency.

If a manservant is doing the whisking he can be lightly flogged at this time even if he doesn't fully deserve it.

Once all of the olive oil has been whisked in add the Meyer lemon juice and continue to whisk. This is a good time to drink a gin and tonic since whisking or watching a person whisk can wear one out.

If Lady Estima Davenport's Mayonnaise is a little bit too thick it can be gently, carefully and lovingly thinned out with a little drizzle of fresh water.

The mayonnaise should immediately be placed in the refrigerator since it is so voluptuously naughty it will be fingered by passers-by or stolen by the French.

The mayonnaise can be used for any dish requiring an aioli like po' boys, smoked oysters and clams, asparagus, fingerling potatoes, grilled prawns, quail and pheasant, and all manner of tasty little sandwiches

Lady Davenport is particularly fond of black garlic mayonnaise and a well-received favorite at Frimley Hall is baked leg of locally sourced rabbit with steamed leeks smothered in it.

Mr. Lesley Merkin's Black Garlic Vinaigrette

Leslie Merkin is the much celebrated owner of The Best Head in The Village Salon in Woollard End where he does all of the nobs including both Lady Estima Davenport and Muriel Dinwiddy and all of the local charity shop Godmothers and soldiers including Marjorie

(Slasher) Cordwangler, Agatha (The Beast) Flange-Gusset, and Mrs. Felicity (Knuckles) Pules.

As a younger chap Miss Merkin was no stranger to the Bloomsbury set, and was a close confidante of Virginia Woolfe, E.M Forster, Lytton Stratchey John Maynard-Keynes, Saxon Sydney-Turney and many others with posh sounding and hyphenated surnames.

He had also been a willing week-end guest with his cousin the noted poetess and welder Ophelia Merkin and the *hoi poloi* of the Bloomsbury self-infatuated coterie fueled by naughty Ottoline Morell, whose estate Garsington was a Bloomsbury knocking-shop of amorous badinage, infatuation, vigorous fingering, plenteous boy-work and not inconsiderable gossipage.

This recipe was suggested to Mr. Leslie by the late Noel Coward who was also no stranger to tossing some fresh leaves with it.

Ingredients:

Half cup roughly chopped freshly sourced cilantro

8 cloves of nicely peeled best black garlic

One third cup of freshly squeezed nice lime juice

One third cup of extra virgin or rarely ever naughty olive oil

One level tablespoon of best white cane sugar

One level teaspoonful of nicely ground coriander

Some Kosher or nun blessed salt

Method:

Combine the ingredients except the salt and the sugar carefully in a nice bowl and blend them together thoroughly with either a whisk or an electric blender. Mr. Leslie of course likes to do everything by hand.

When nicely blended and all gooey slowly add the salt and sugar tasting very regularly until seasoning is exactly to your liking.

Place in the refrigerator and check for Dutch people who will try to filch it and attempt to sell it to the French.

Drink two gin and tonics.

Mr. Leslie enjoys this vinaigrette on all manner of salads which he eats frequently to keep himself nice and trim for both Maypole and Morris Dancing.

He particularly enjoys it with a dish of delightfully shaved fresh beetroot or with fire roasted peppers.

It was claimed that some of the Bloomsbury set carried sterling silver flasks of black garlic vinaigrette for 'special' occasions since it was believed by some of the naughtier faction that it had aphrodisiac qualities.

Mrs. Misaki Fong's Black Garlic Shrimp with Roasted Asparagus

It was exceptionally rare for there to be any Japanese visitors to Woollard End although industrialist Hirohito Fong was an exception. Local imbecile Mrs. Tippy Horseposture had opened up a tree climbing goat farm at nearby Sandon Bottom having successfully cultivated there the exceptional *argania spinosa* (Argan trees), normally endemic to the calcereous semi-desert Sous Valley of South Western Morocco.

Tamri goats are oddly seduced by the berries of Argan trees and are adept at climbing them to get at the naughty fruit. The tree climbing Tamri Goat's droppings contain seed kernels which can be ground into an oil that is used in both cooking and cosmetics. Tippy's mother, who had many years previously owned a cookie shop in Woollard End called A Gal Named Millie's Biscottis had a twice baked cookie recipe that Tippy had attempted using the oil she had abstracted from Tamri Goat droppings.

To cut a long story short the new cookie was entirely indestructible and the recipe was purchased by Mr. Fong who had used it to manufacture the construction material 'fongite'.

That Old Black Garlic Has Me In Its Spell

The 1,245 feet tall Fong Tower in Fukuoka on the northern shore of the island of Kyushu is built entirely from fongite which could withstand both the severest of earthquakes and a major nuclear event.

Mrs. Misaki Fong visited Woollard End with her diminutive yellow husband Hirohito 'Shorty' Fong and having obtained some black garlic from noted local market gardener Quimbush Merkin employed the same in her spectacular recipe.

Ingredients:

12 cloves carefully peeled black garlic

12 big plump naughty shrimp carefully peeled and de-veined

1 pound of freshly sourced and cleaned asparagus with the nasty woody bits removed

1 teaspoon of kosher or nun blessed salt

I teaspoon of freshly ground pink

peppercorns

1 tablespoon of carefully chopped fresh ginger root avoiding the nasty old woody bits

Half a cup of sweetish Sake (drink other half of cup)

1 teaspoon of your favorite sriracha sauce

1 tablespoon of extra virgin or only very occasionally naughty olive oil

Method:

Make a lovely marinade by combining everything except the shrimp and the asparagus using a food processor, a stick blender, or an indentured servant who can be lightly flogged at regular yet appropriate intervals.

This will produce a silky smooth puree a small part of which should be reserved in the refrigerator to use as a dressing when the dish is served to your drooling guests (two or three tablespoons should suffice).

Take the plump naughty shrimp and slosh the marinade mixture over them in a bowl until they are well-covered. Mrs. Fong claims she can actually hear the shrimp purr with crustaceous delight as they bathe seductively in the mixture.

Cover the bowl and let the marinade do its sexy work in a refrigerator for fifty minutes or so.

Drink at least three gin and tonics while you are waiting.

Turn on your oven and set at 400 degrees

Twirl and flounce the prepared asparagus with the extra virgin (or only very occasionally naughty) olive oil together with the salt and ground pink peppercorns until they are all lovely and moistened and then place seductively in your nicest roasting pan.

Make sure your oven is at 400 degrees.

Roast for 12 minutes, remove and keep nice and warm.

Cook your marinated shrimp in a favorite skillet over a goodly heat flipping them after two minutes or so. They should tremble with delight when perfectly done.

Drink a gin and tonic.

Lay your warm asparagus on your best porcelain plates nicely (the dish will keep hotter on porcelain) and quickly arrange your sexy black garlic marinated shrimp on top.

Drizzle with the reserved sauce and gobble noisily with a nice bottle or two Pinot Grigio or Sauvignon Blanc.

That Old Black Garlic Has Me In Its Spell

Stumble down to Ye Olde Black Pig in Woollard End or other favorite moistening establishment and tell the locals how good your dinner was.

That part of Suffolk was no stranger to fine dining with Ye Olde Black Pig and nearby Sandon Bottom's Slug and Lettuce both considered as gourmet havens.

Amitrasudan 'Ernie' Bhagwat's Black Garlic Infused Curried Lamb

Amitrasudan 'Ernie' Bhagwat was a living legend in Woollard End for both his very superior news agency work and his foul language.

His coming to Woollard End was shrouded in mystery... but here goes.

Amitrasudan Bhagwat, whose Indian first name translated as 'destroyer of enemies', was an exceptionally genial fellow who had come to Woollard End as a boy concealed by his parents in the luggage of noted local good old boy Bunty Frobisher just before Bunty's return from doing something terribly clerical for the Raj in Bombay.

Bunty lived in the newly converted old stable block at the impressive county pile that was Woodruffe Hall
The Bhagwat's had provided ample food and drink for their shiny brown spawn who came to learn English through the air holes bored through Bunty Frobisher's largest suitcase during the fifty-eight day sea voyage.

That Old Black Garlic Has Me In Its Spell

Unfortunately the ripeness of the expletives of the various foul-mouthed seafaring men who couldn't work out just where the small cans of ablutions in the luggage hold were coming from provided little Amitrasudan with the vocabulary of a Spittlefield's meat cutter.

Bunty Frobisher himself had found the little tike fast asleep in his largest suitcase when he was supervising his unpacking at Woodruffe Hall. The little fellow soon awoke and greeted Frobisher's faithful old manservant Quizzling with a shrill "How's your cock mate?'

Bunty, no stranger to a bucket or two of gin in the forenoons out in the steaming colonies, certainly didn't recall packing a small boy in with his cricket gear and polo equipment, although he vaguely remembered taking something on account of his snooker winnings.

He also recalled that Lady Davenport had won her aged and now feeble gardener old Mr. Sachs from Lady Felicia Tumblemore at a bridge tournament.

Bunty did the right thing of course and kept the little fellow at Woodruffe Hall and put the now styled 'Ernie' Bhagwat through news agency school.

Years later, when old Basil Fudge, who had been the news agent in Woollard End for over fifty years, finally gave up the ghost, Ernie took over, with the help of a tasty little inheritance he had been bequeathed from The Frobisher Estate.

Once, at the annual Woollard End Talent Contest in The Rudyard Kipling Village Hall, he appearance as Tennessee Ernie Bhagwat wearing unnecessarily tight leather trousers and accompanying himself on an electric sitar.

His rendition of Peggy Singh brought the house down, most particularly when he had thrown his immaculately laundered handkerchief courtesy of Mrs. Nana Poonani's Wishy Washy Laundry to the ladies rapturously moistening in the front row.

One had actually exclaimed quite loudly that she had always assumed that circumcision was universal in the Indian sub-continent.

Almost immediately Ernie started to do well in news agency he had brought his very aged parents over from Bombay and they now resided over the shop.

The marvelous aromas of Mrs. Indira Bhagwat's goat saagwala and her lovely aloo tikki with chola wafted invitingly down Kipling Avenue bringing back to dear old

Blighty fond memories to the several old buffers and their memsahibs who had spent time blundering around in The Raj and being surly to the indigenous brownish folk.

One of Mrs. Bhagwat's most wondrous creations (now perfected by Ernie) was her fabled black garlic infused curried lamb

Ingredients:

4 teaspoons naughty minced black garlic
One and a half pounds of best trimmed boneless lamb cut into one inch cubes
Quarter cup of best vegetable oil
3 bay leaves
One and a half level teaspoons of best Garam Masala
1 and a half cups off freshly diced (not canned) tomato
Half a cup of plain yoghurt
3 tablespoons chopped cilantro (fresh)
1 finely chopped red chili
1 cardamon pod

That Old Black Garlic Has Me In Its Spell

Kosher or nun blessed salt

Half a teaspoon of powdered tumeric (careful! it will stain stuff)

1 smallish stick of cinnamon

12 black or green peppercorns

1 whole clove

One and a half finely chopped yellow or white onions

1 tablespoon fresh finely chopped ginger (no woody bits)

1 level teaspoon of corander powder

1 level teaspoon smoked cayenne powder

Juice of half a fresh lime

Method:

Heat vegetable oil in your favorite large pan; add bay leaves, cardamom, cinnamon, peppercorns (black or green), and clove.

When it all begins to smell all lovely add the onions and cook slowly without burning until all are wilted and naughty and golden brown (a bit over ten minutes should suffice) keep stirring enough to prevent any sticking or burning.

Drink a cold Indian Pale Ale or at a push a nice large gin and tonic

Carefully add the ginger paste, garlic, chili pepper, and trimmed and cubed lamb.

Carefully season cubed lamb with kosher or nun blessed salt and gently sizzle it all nicely in the pan stirring regularly for about twenty-five minutes more.

If the dish begins to dry a little and annoyingly stick add a little warmed water to the pan

Carefully add the spices (Garam Masala, cayenne, turmeric, and coriander) stirring as necessary and moisten with a little more water if necessary and adding non-canned tomatoes (to avoid the nasty tinny taste)and

continue to stir and let the dish bubble
gently away.

Add more water to the pan (about three or
so cups should do nicely) and bubble away
happily for about fifteen more minutes after
which the lamb should be almost tender
enough to gobble up.

When almost done perfectly stir in the
yoghurt without bruising it and let simmer
gently until perfectly cooked with a nice
naughty thick black garlic and curry sauce.

Drink a gin and tonic or a second India
Pale Ale and quickly garnish the dish with a
sprinkling of the nice, fresh cilantro and a
drizzle of lime juice.

Serve with spicy poppadums and your
favorite Indian side-dish together with both
perfectly steamed Basmati rice and your
favorite dear old Nan.

Have some lovely lime or lemon pickle and a bucket of mango chutney standing by.

Ghandi is a jolly good film to watch while eating this delightful repast although the film lasts a little over nine hours.

Ernie Bhagwat was an extra in the movie and is in the 452nd row back in the funeral procession,

This meal is hugely enjoyed by the many elderly former administrators of the British Raj who have now retired to Woollard End and now hunt rabbits and squirrels with a van instead of tigers from atop an elephant.

Muriel Dinwiddy's Most Excellent Black Garlic Rubbed Sea Bass in a Parcel

Local tennis celebrity Muriel Dinwiddy (82) (nee Fotheringay) is the old school chum and tennis partner of Lady Estima Davenport.

Ms. Dinwiddy is very fold of rabbit hunting although she now secretly releases them unharmed into the Woollard Public Library to annoy Library Director Miss Myngge following a lengthy dispute over an overdue book fine. She despised the French having once claimed, "I had rather a provocative glance from a French person in Fortnum and Mason's while I was purchasing a pound of cheese...nothing French of course...Sage? Derby?...or maybe it was Shropshire Blue? The French are always so peculiarly shifty looking I have always thought ... especially around our cheeses. They most likely steal our sheep too, so very ungentlemanly, we should still hang them."

Muriel Dinwiddy had received a lengthy training as a nurse during the Second and with Estima Davenport had spent some time at Bletchley Park with MI5 Muriel had actually broken the Enigma Code.

It was indeed she rather than the oft credited Polish Cipher Bureau. Muriel's break through was based not on theoretical

That Old Black Garlic Has Me In Its Spell

mathematics but rather on the variable gestation periods of certain rare fruit annoying aphids.

Ingredients:

1 nice juicy fillet of a fresh sea bass (check the eyes and gills for freshness)
1 teaspoon of best light soy sauce

One third of a teaspoon finely chopped fresh lemongrass (avoid woody bits)
Two tablespoons of your best dry sherry or even white port
1 finely chopped scallion
2 clove cloves of carefully peeled and then finely chopped black garlic
One quarter of a teaspoon of carefully grated fresh ginger (no woody bits) grated

Sliced fresh Meyer lemon for garnish

A handful of fresh watercress for garnish

1 teaspoon fresh cilantro (chopped) for a nice bright garnish

Method:

Preheat your spotless oven to 375 degrees.

Using your nicest bowl, mix the soy sauce, ginger, lemongrass, and naughty black garlic into a nice gooey paste.

Carefully lay you lovely plump fresh fillet of sea bass on some nice clean aluminum foil.

Lovingly rub the gooey paste all over the sea bass fingering it gently as necessary. It may squeal slightly with delight.

Drizzle your sherry or white port (a little sweeter) over the rubbed and lightly fingered sea bass.

Carefully sprinkle the chopped scallion

on top of the nicely moistened bass.

Make a nice parcel by carefully folding the foil around the expectant bass.

Bake for 12-14 minutes making sure it is fully cooked

Carefully take the bass from its comfy parcel, reserving the lovely liquid.

Serve on your finest porcelain platter (it will keep much hotter) sprinkled with cilantro and juices from the parcel and garnish with some slices of the Meyer lemon and surround with the watercress.

Muriel Dinwiddy usually serves her sea bass with grilled asparagus and buttered fingerling potatoes sprinkled with fresh parsley and grated pink peppercorns.

A nice locally sourced dry cider is an

ideal accompaniment. The thirty-seven percent proof Woodruffe's Best Cider (brewed in Woollard End since 1342) is best avoided because of issues involving blindness.

Sidney 'Porky' Widgeon's Bangers with Black Garlic and Onion Gravy

Widgeons' Family Butchers had been

purveyors of fresh meat, fish and game to the gentlefolk of Woollard End since 1456.

The present principal of the firm is the notably stout Sidney Widgeon aided by his equally plump and near imbecile spawn Sidney junior. Junior regularly had his shiny delivery tricycle with its huge basket on the front filched by the rascals and oiks of Caligula House at the local public school St. Humbert's.

Redoubtable Butcher Widgeon was Vice-Captain of Woollard End Cricket XI (known for his donkey drop bowling), Co-Captain of Ye Old Black Pig Shove Ha'penny Team, Chairman of The Woollard End Parish Council's Sub-Committee for Pub Snacks Pickles, Jellied Eels and Potato Chips (crisps), double gold medal winner in the European Hog

Trussing Championships beating out plucky Frenchman Jean-Claude Le Touch on both occasions.

Expert trussing is essential to pork butchering and according to E.F. Dalrymple's *Principles of Hog Trussing* (1892) "One's hog must never be given the opportunity to tumble from the spit into the fire pit thus trussing must be both aggressive and tight".

Widgeon was both a magnificent hog trusser as his many international victories will attest and he is also a most accomplished pig roaster and his award winning methodology is as follows.

1. Slide the spit decorously between the thighs along the inside of the carcass just under the hog's spine and through the mouth.

2. Using a patent trussing needle

(Chalcedony's No 2 is best) and the heaviest duty (industrial strength) kitchen twine secure the spit to the spine (or vice versa) every six inches or so along the hog carcass. Make sure the knots are very tightly tied (see, *Scouting for Girls, Official Handbook of the Girl Scouts: Knots, Splices and Rope Work: A Practical Treatise*). Make sure excess twine is snipped off so it will not burn and impair flavor.

3. The hog's comely thighs, hips, and legs together with the head and shoulders must be securely trussed against each other to prevent any wiggle and or waggle.

Your hog is now as ready as it will ever be ready for roasting.

Roasting your hog - Widgeon's methodology

Prepare your fire pit with your favorite coals, wood, etc. Light fire for the roasting to at least 250 degrees or so.

Arrange for the youths working in relays to

gently rotate the hog on the spit for 18-24 hours or so. This is tiring work so ensure a St. John's Ambulance is standing by, and ensure parents know where their male spawn are. Have plenty of bandages and suitable salves and ointments available.

Using a new mop regularly and carefully slosh some of the basting liquids over the hog when a hint of dryness is spotted. A puny and somewhat thoughtful youth makes an ideal dryness spotter. This vital activity will both comfort the hog, ensure full flavor, and prevent the hog's burning. Make sure the basting liquid is well stirred particularly so that the sugar ingredient does not serve to char the exterior

Check the internal temperature of the hog as it approaches your desired doneness using a meat thermometer (Flange and Sunbeam's No.5 Meat Thermometer is best.) Ideally the deepest meat should be about 165 degrees Fahrenheit. Check the youths for burns, apply ointments and bandages as necessary, give them each a shilling and send them on their way.

Ingredients for Bangers:

12 ounces nice lean pork preferably organic, minced
4 ounces lovely plump pork belly, minced
2 ounces fresh white breadcrumbs
1 white onion, peeled & grated
1/2 lemon rind (zesty) finely grated
A little pinch of finely grated Nutmeg
1 teaspoon chopped curly parsley
2 teaspoons of fresh herbs (sage, thyme and marjoram)-at a pinch dried herbs will work but only one teaspoon
1 teaspoon freshly ground black or white pepper
Kosher (or nun blessed) salt to taste
2 nice brown free range eggs vigorously

beaten

Half tablespoon flour

1 nice brown egg white

1 ounce best butter

1 tablespoon light oil

Method for Bangers:

Combine all the lovely naughty fresh meats with the fresh breadcrumbs, grated white onion, lemon rind, nutmeg, parsley, fresh or dried herbs, pepper & salt. Mix well. It is better (and far more pleasing) to mix this together with your hands using vigorous fingering as necessary.

Bind with the 2 beaten eggs & mix well again.

Chill the sausage mixture in the fridge - it will easier to handle when it is slightly firmer. You can also use the mixture for stuffing a bird (if she lets you) at this stage too.

Drink a gin and tonic or even two at a pinch.

When you are ready to cook the sausages form the mixture into sausage shapes - using a little flour to help you.

Dip the sausages into the beaten egg white and then dust lightly with the flour and set aside until you are ready to use them.

Heat the oil and butter together in a large frying pan (deep sided is better since they like to spit a little) and cook the happy sizzling naughty sausages for about 10-15 minutes over a medium heat.

Turn them regularly to ensure they brown evenly. This browning makes them more pleasing in appearance. They will sometimes squeal with pleasure at this point.

Drain them on a paper towel & serve hot over lovely horseradish mashed potatoes liberally sploshed all over with lashings of red onion, black garlic and sherry gravy for a delightful "Bangers & Mash" supper.

Have lots of scrumptious Coleman's mustard at the ready.

Ingredients for Red Onion Black Garlic and Sherry gravy:

A big dollop of butter

Six nice big juicy cloves of carefully peeled black garlic

Two large red onions, peeled and very thinly sliced

A level tablespoon of flour

That Old Black Garlic Has Me In Its Spell

1/3 of a cup of cooking sherry

1 and a half cups of beef or chicken stock

A little dribble of Worcestershire sauce

Method:

Melt the butter in a heavy pan, throw in the thinly sliced onions and the garlic carefully sliced and cook gently over a low heat till sexily dark reddish gold and soft. Be careful not to burn them. Even the French won't eat them burnt.

Continue cooking, covered with a lid until the onions are truly deep purple-reddish brown and soft enough to squish between your fingers (take care to let them cool before checking for degree of squish.)

Stir into the nicely reposing onions a level heaped tablespoon of flour and cook slowly for a few minutes until all is lightly browned.

Pour in the liquids. Season with salt and pepper and Worcestershire sauce and bring to a slow boil.

Turn down the heat so that the gravy bubbles nicely and gently and leave for about fifteen minutes, stirring from time to time.

Adjust seasoning to taste

Pour gently into your best porcelain gravy boat (especially 18th century Worcester or Bow) and use scrumptiously as required over your bangers and horseradish mashed potatoes. Yum.

ABOUT THE AUTHOR

Keith Pepperell grew up in Woollard End but who now lives in East Seepage KY is a near simpleton who can often be seen on TV pretending to be an historian. He has written over forty dull books all of which have tumbled still born from the presses. He knows almost nothing about food and constantly complains in restaurants to the annoyance of those around him. He has made a number of documentary films and these days hardly ever cross-dresses. He once pretended to be blind to get an earlier flight and was embarrassed when he got the flight and was also bumped up to first class. The airline sent his luggage to Belgium. proving 'mysterious ways'.